JOHN FISHER

JOHN FISHER

A Lecture delivered in the Hall of
St John's College on the occasion
of the Quatercentenary Celebration
by Queens', Christ's, St John's and
Trinity Colleges

by

E. A. BENIANS, M.A.
Master of St John's College

Wednesday, 24 July 1935

CAMBRIDGE
AT THE UNIVERSITY PRESS
1935

CAMBRIDGE
UNIVERSITY PRESS

University Printing House, Cambridge CB2 8BS, United Kingdom

Published in the United States of America by Cambridge University Press, New York

Cambridge University Press is part of the University of Cambridge.

It furthers the University's mission by disseminating knowledge in the pursuit of
education, learning and research at the highest international levels of excellence.

www.cambridge.org
Information on this title: www.cambridge.org/9781107640627

© Cambridge University Press 1935

First published 1935
Re-issued 2014

A catalogue record for this publication is available from the British Library

ISBN 978-1-107-64062-7 Paperback

JOHN FISHER

Four colleges unite to-day to pay homage to the memory of John Fisher. In the noble list of founders and benefactors which our University and our colleges preserve, few names stand out with the eminence of his.

He was Master of Michaelhouse and President of Queens' College; and, with the Lady Margaret, a founder of Christ's College and St John's. In the University he held the offices of Senior Proctor, Lady Margaret Professor, Vice-Chancellor and Chancellor—that of Chancellor for thirty-one years.

In the early sixteenth century, when kings still went on pilgrimage, Henry VII set out for the shrine of St Mary at Walsingham. On his way he visited Cambridge. The University received him with all its ancient ceremony. The four orders of friars, the other religious orders and all the graduates according to their degrees awaited him. At the University Cross the King alighted and there Doctor Fisher, then Chancellor of the University (it was the year 1506), accompanied by other doctors, made 'a little proposition' and welcomed him.[1]

The 'little proposition' was a lengthy oration in Latin.[2] Somewhat fanciful in its account of the past glories of Cambridge, it yet contains a passage that illuminates for us the last years of the medieval University. We were in the depths of misfortune, said the Chancellor, when Your Majesty first came to our aid; continual strife with the townsmen, the long abiding of the plague and the want of benefactors had brought almost all of us to a weariness of learning. Many were planning to depart at the first opportunity. With your coming the sun has risen upon us.

The picture was a little overcharged with gloom, for Fisher had himself contributed to appease the strife with the town, and the records of the University show no decline in its activities in these years.[3] But new benefactions were bitterly needed, and the orator

[1] Cooper, C. H., *Annals of Cambridge*, I, 281.
[2] Printed in Lewis, J., *Life of Dr John Fisher*, II, 263–72.
[3] Grace Book B, Part I, p. xxvi.

was leading up to his final theme—the unfinished college of Henry VI—'a work for thee divinely destined' to complete. Did Fisher, when he spoke thus, know of the king's intentions? We cannot say. But before King Henry died he made provision for the perfect finishing of the chapel, which Fisher lived to see.

The procession moved on to the lodge of Queens' College, where royal visitors were accustomed to stay, and of which Fisher had become President in the preceding year.

At the time of this royal visit Fisher was midway in his career, about thirty-seven years of age, of which some twenty-three had been spent in Cambridge. His earliest biographer describes him as tall and comely, six feet in height, upright and well-framed, 'somewhat wide-mouthed and big-jawed, as one ordained to utter speech much', and grave in countenance.[1] He had that asset of authority, a powerful voice, and when moved his manner could be vehement. Erasmus said of him that when he warmed to the contest he could not

[1] *The Life of Fisher* (MS. Harleian 6382), Early English Text Society, pp. 129–30.

easily desist[1]—a judgment Fisher's life was to illustrate. Already he had become the leading spirit in the University.

Born at Beverley in Yorkshire in 1469,[2] the eldest child of a prosperous merchant, he had been educated at the school attached to the Collegiate Church and had come up to Michaelhouse, a boy of fourteen. We have but glimpses of his student days—a grateful tribute to the exact teaching in geometry, given by his old tutor, William de Melton,[3] and a wish, expressed long after, that the text books in logic and rhetoric had been more attractive.[4] 'We were scholars together in Cambridge', wrote the Carthusian, John Bouge, 'and for a little pastime I might speak to him out of my chamber window into his chamber window.'[5] Seven years of study were required to make a

[1] *Erasmi Epistolae*, ed. Allen, P. S., IV, 73.

[2] Lloyd, A. H., *Early History of Christ's College*, p. 391. Dr Lloyd kindly sent me a transcript of the dispensation to Fisher in 1491 which he has discovered in the Papal Archives. (*Reg. Later.* 908, f. 70). In this Fisher's age is given as twenty-two.

[3] Bridgett, T. E., *Life of Blessed John Fisher*, p. 12. See *Jo. Fischerii Opera* (1597), col. 1128. [4] *Erasmi Epist.* II, 90.

[5] *English Works of Sir Thomas More*, ed. Campbell, W. E., II[1].

master. Fisher became questionist in 1488, was soon after elected a Fellow of Michael-house, and proceeded to the Master's degree in 1491. He had evidently made some mark, for three years later he was appointed Senior Proctor in the University,[1] an office next in importance to that of Vice-Chancellor. The proctors were generally young men; they were the maids-of-all-work of the University, and their multifarious duties demanded energy and competence. When Melton resigned the Mastership of Michaelhouse in 1497, Fisher succeeded him.

The appointment as Senior Proctor was a turning-point in his life. In 1495 University business took him to the Court at Greenwich. 'I dined', wrote Fisher, 'with the Lady mother of the King.'[2] Thus began an acquaintance of memorable consequence to both. Seven years later the Lady Margaret made him her Chaplain and Confessor. 'She chose me', he wrote, 'as her director...to guide her life, yet I gladly confess that I learnt more from her virtue than ever I could teach her.'[3] Fisher

[1] Grace Book B, Part I, p. 67. [2] *Ibid.* p. 68.
[3] *Opera*, p. 747.

(9)

had thus the opportunity to direct her bounty towards those needs of the University on which his mind was fixed. Meanwhile he had pursued the arduous course for the doctorate in Theology and had become Vice-Chancellor.[1]

Cambridge had by this time risen from the obscurity of a local reputation to take her place by the side of her older sister as a national University. Numbers had grown rapidly during the latter half of the fifteenth century and towards its close nearly equalled the diminished numbers of Oxford.[2] Schools of Divinity, Arts and Civil Law had arisen, the University Library had been founded and a new University Church was building. By this time, too, the College system was firmly established. From its earliest expression in the famous rule of Merton, the idea of the college had been progressively expanded and was reaching its modern form—the community of scholars, living under discipline, in a house that rivalled in splendour the great monastic houses, taught within the college

[1] Grace Book B, Part I, pp. 143, 162.
[2] Rashdall, H., *Universities of Europe*, II, 553.

walls and including in their number students not on the foundation. Colleges stretched in an almost continuous line from Peterhouse to King's Hall. The college had learned much from the monastery, but its purpose was different. The monastery formed a body of recluses; the college sent forth a trained clergy for service in Church and State. Hence its appeal to Fisher.

The scholar in a college was under supervision and restraint, but he had a home of reasonable comfort. He was no longer tempted to enter one of the religious houses, so prominent in medieval Cambridge, or left at the mercy of 'practised extortioners'. But only a privileged minority of the students were in colleges. Others lived a less disciplined life in the hostels, whose brawlings so frequently disturbed the peace.

While these material changes were strengthening the University, on the intellectual side it was hardly touched by the stir of a new age. When Fisher graduated a printed book was still almost a curiosity.[1] Greek learning was unknown. The scholastic discipline was firmly

[1] Grace Book A, p. xliv.

entrenched and Church and University stood together in its defence. The art of reasoning had been cultivated to perfection, and talented young men won their degrees by prolonged and subtle disputations in Latin, supporting their arguments from the Bible, the Fathers, the medieval commentators and the Canon Law. Fisher was bred in this system. He was not a Humanist and the spirit of Humanism is sought in vain in his writings. But he saw in the improvement of education the way of advance to a more spiritual religion. Thus would the Church be reformed and the evils of the time banished. A man of deep piety, he found little comfort either at home or abroad. Abroad the rise of a Moslem power oppressed his mind. 'Our religion of Christian faith is greatly diminished', he said in a sermon in 1507, 'we be very few.'[1] At home he condemned the worldliness of the clergy. 'In that time', he says, speaking of the early Church, 'were no chalices of gold, but then was many golden priests, now be many chalices of gold and almost no golden priests.'[2]

[1] *English Works of John Fisher*, ed. Mayor, J. E. B., p. 171.
[2] *Ibid.* p. 181.

An educated, preaching priesthood was one of the needs of England which the University might satisfy. But without new foundations learning would remain in the old channels.

Medieval piety turned instinctively to the endowment of religious houses, whence perpetual prayers might rise for the good of the donor's soul. Fisher essayed to show the Lady Margaret how by serving learning she could serve religion too. A scholar herself, her sympathies could be won for the Universities. The schools of learning, he told her, were meanly endowed, the provisions for scholars were very few and small, and colleges were yet wanting for their maintenance. What more meritorious than to educate a multitude of young men in learning and virtue, who should carry the gospel through all the bounds of Britain.[1]

The great benefactions of the Lady Margaret to the University began with a perpetual public lectureship in Divinity, since called the Lady Margaret Professorship. Established

[1] Baker, T., *History of the College of St John the Evangelist*, p. 59; Hymers, J., *Funeral Sermon of Margaret Countess of Richmond*, Appendix No. 10, Letter to the University, pp. 220–1.

in 1501, it was the beginning for Cambridge of the professorial system. In the medieval University the regent masters and doctors gathered students round them and were paid by their fees. That system was slowly replaced by lecturers endowed from University funds and college resources. Fisher, appointed in 1502, was the first holder of the new office. The reader was required to lecture daily in the Divinity Schools without fee, except during Lent, when he and his class might devote themselves to preaching.

During the latter Middle Ages the sermon had fallen into disfavour in the Church, but Fisher saw in the revival of preaching a weapon of reform, and in 1504 the Lady Margaret Preachership followed the Lady Margaret Professorship. Something had thus been done to provide gratuitous instruction in theology in the University and preaching in the vernacular. Fisher himself was a leader in the reform of the pulpit. A high authority attributes to him 'the most finished pulpit eloquence' of that day,[1] and two of his ser-

[1] Hitchcock, E. V. and Chambers, R. W., *Harpsfield's Life of Sir Thomas More*, E.E.T.S., p. cliv.

mons, those on King Henry VII and the Lady Margaret, live in the history of English prose.

University distinction was a recognised passport to public service. The Chancellor of the University at the time was Richard Foxe, Bishop of Durham, 'a wise man' Bacon calls him,[1] and the King's most trusted minister. He took a warm interest in Fisher, and Fisher gratefully acknowledges the inspiration that as a young man he received from Foxe.[2] Foxe did not believe in men lingering in the University. He recommended Fisher for promotion and in 1504 the King offered Fisher the Bishopric of Rochester. Rumour attributed this advancement to the Lady Margaret's influence, but Fisher, who always owned his debt to her in other ways, was at pains to deny this[3] and the King's own letter to his mother is clear evidence to the contrary.[4] The appointment was a good one and Fisher's discharge of his episcopal duties was singularly conscientious.

[1] *Life of Henry VII* (ed. 1870), p. 302.
[2] Bridgett, T. E., *op. cit.* p. 25. See *Opera*, p. 746.
[3] *Opera*, p. 746. See also *Vie du bienheureux martyr Jean Fisher*, ed. Van Ortroy, S.J., p. 93.
[4] Printed in Hymers, J., *op. cit.*, Appendix No. 1, p. 163.

He now resigned the Mastership of Michael-house, but he remained Chancellor of the University, to which office he was elected in this year. For a great part of the fifteenth century the Chancellors had been residents, generally heads of colleges. But the growing public business of the University was henceforth to make rank and power more important than residence in the choice of a Chancellor. The change was to have its political risks for the University. Fisher was but the first of five Cambridge Chancellors of the sixteenth century who perished on the scaffold.

Rochester was not too far from Cambridge for Fisher to keep in touch with the University. But it was also near to London. Episcopal duties and private studies, he complained, were too frequently interrupted by a message from the Court to 'attend such a triumph or public entry or receive such an ambassador',[1] though politics and pomp were distasteful to him and the expenses taxed a slender income. The palace did not realise Erasmus's standard of comfort. Its draughts and marshy airs he found unbearable. But Fisher passed many of

[1] Lewis, J., *op. cit.* I, 70.

his happiest hours in the famous library he collected there.[1]

Before he removed to Rochester an important project was engaging his attention at Cambridge. The College of Godshouse dated back to 1439. First founded by William Byngham, a London rector, as a college for the training of grammar school masters, it was refounded by Henry VI. It was almost the poorest of the colleges, and to its needs Fisher had directed the attention of the Lady Margaret. She, for the love that she bore her uncle King Henry VI, desired to complete his work and to refound the college as a larger society under a new name. In his *Early History of Christ's College*, Dr Lloyd has shown the close relations in University business that had existed between Fisher and John Sycling, the Proctor of Godshouse, and in urging the claims of Godshouse Fisher may well have been influenced by this friendship.[2]

In the foundation of Christ's College the Lady Margaret took a personal part, which her death in 1509 prevented in the case of St John's.

[1] *Erasmi Epist.* v, 536–7.
[2] Lloyd, A. H., *op. cit.* pp. 281–3.

But for the new statutes Fisher had the prime responsibility. It is characteristic of him that they both follow the old and flow into more detail. Prominence was given to the original purpose of Godshouse—the training of grammar school masters; and original features in the old statutes were preserved, as, for example, the institution of the college lecturer, the admission of pensioners, and the provision for the study of the poets and orators of antiquity.[1] Thus Byngham's ideas were made effective by Fisher in a stronger society. Devotion to the Church never obliterated in Fisher the local attachments of the Englishman, and the interest that both he and the Lady Margaret felt in their own part of England appears in the provision that of the twelve Fellows at least half should be chosen from the nine northern counties—a preference given them, amongst other reasons, on account of their poverty. In October 1506 the thrice-founded college began its existence under its new name. Fisher was made Visitor for life and the college gratefully remembered by an annual dirge his

[1] Rackham, H., *Early Statutes of Christ's College*, p. 149; Lloyd, A. H., *op. cit.* pp. 298–300.

influence used on its behalf, his gifts for its adornment and his wise legislation.[1]

It was while engaged in these duties that Fisher became President of Queens'. The Lady Margaret had assumed the royal interest in that college and, at her request, Thomas Wilkinson resigned the Presidency in April 1505 and the Fellows elected Fisher to succeed him. As we shall see, Fisher desired to have a home in Cambridge, but not the responsible charge of a college. Yet we may judge from the letters of the Fellows, when he resigned his post in 1508, that he had taken a close interest in its affairs. They asked him to nominate his successor, writing to the Lady Margaret, 'if we might not continue with him, at least by his appointment we should have such one as somewhat should assemble him and his goodly and godly manners.'[2] He chose for them a Fellow of his own college, Michaelhouse, Dr Bekensaw.

Before Christ's College had been formally opened Fisher was contemplating another and larger foundation. When the idea of suppress-

[1] Rackham, H., *op. cit.* pp. 126–33.
[2] Searle, W. G., *History of the Queens' College*, p. 140.

ing the hospital of St John the Evangelist in favour of a college of secular students first occurred to him, we do not know, but the matter was discussed in the Lady Margaret's Council as early as 1505.[1] Suggestions were being pressed upon her that the other University ought this time to benefit by her favours, but Fisher's advice prevailed.[2] The brethren of the hospital enjoyed the privileges of the University, but had no part, like the other religious orders, in its life and functions. Their number had come down at this time to three, and their conduct of their affairs showed that they had learned little from the fate of St Rhadegund's.

In March 1509 the Lady Margaret entered into an agreement with the Bishop of Ely, her step-son, for the suppression of the hospital, and she arranged to endow the new college from her lands in Devon, Somerset and Northamptonshire. Henry VII died in April 1509, and the Lady Margaret in June, before further steps were taken, and the proposed disposition of her property was not legally

[1] Scott, Sir R. F., *Records of St John's College*, IV, 204.
[2] Baker, T., *op. cit.* pp. 59–60.

secure. Her purpose could only be effected with the new King's favour. Fisher looked hopefully to one 'endued', as he said, 'with all graces of God and nature and with as great habylytees and likelihoods of well doing as ever was in King'.[1] The licence to found the college was promptly granted; the property was another question. Around Henry were influences as hostile to the pious liberality of his grandmother as to the closefistedness of his father. Fisher soon found himself involved in a struggle with squalid interests and baffling delays that taxed all the skill and tenacity of his nature. The foundation of Christ's College, with the Court on his side, and a wise friend like Sycling to prompt and co-operate, may well have been a pleasant task. Before St John's was founded Fisher, worn out with legal delays, had written: 'Many times I was right sorry that ever I took that business upon me.'[2]

With the death of his step-mother the Bishop of Ely changed his mind, and, on the plea that he had not sealed his agreement, re-

[1] *English Works of John Fisher*, p. 285.
[2] Scott, Sir R. F., *op. cit.* IV, 210.

fused to perform his part. 'This', wrote Fisher, 'was the first sore brunt that we had and like to have quelled all the matter.'[1] On the advice of Foxe, Fisher came to terms with him, and a bargain was struck by which the Bishop was to nominate three Fellows of the college and his successors one. Twice recourse had to be made to Rome, but at last Julius II loosed the papal thunders against the brethren who clung to their living in the old house. Meanwhile the Lady Margaret's will was the subject of interminable proceedings in Chancery, and a storm arose amongst her household, who accused Fisher of robbing them, though he had in fact protected their interests.[2] Then all was interrupted by a royal command to Fisher to attend the Lateran Council in Rome. Fisher made his preparations to go and intended taking Erasmus as secretary.[3] One may wonder what he would have thought of Rome in the pontificate of Leo X, when art sat in the seat of faith. But the royal order was countermanded and Fisher had no part in that

[1] Scott, Sir R. F., *op. cit.* IV, 209.
[2] *Ibid.* p. 210.
[3] *Ibid.* pp. 210–11.

last abortive effort to reform the Church before the Reformation.

After long delays and with much expense, possession of the hospital was obtained in January 1511; in April, the charter of the foundation was granted. 800,000 bricks were ordered from Greenwich and the building of the first court began.[1] The University showed its friendly interest by a grace exempting Dr Shorton, the first Master, from his academic duties.[2] In June 1516 Fisher writes to Erasmus: 'I am getting ready to go to Cambridge for the college is at last to be opened.'[3] The formal opening took place that summer. As for the estates of the Lady Margaret, after many efforts Fisher abandoned hope. The King took the lands as heir-at-law. But some compensation was granted in the confiscated property of three religious houses. To save the college from the poverty which now threatened, Fisher flung his own resources into the struggle and endowed it with a large sum of money given him by the Lady Margaret

[1] Scott, Sir R. F., *op. cit.* IV, 2–3.
[2] Grace Book Γ, p. 100.
[3] *Erasmi Epist.* II, 268.

shortly before her death.[1] Happily, in his archdeacon, Nicholas Metcalfe, probably like himself a member of Michaelhouse, Fisher found for it a third Master, who, in the words of Fuller, 'knew how to make a little College a great one'.[2] Working together the two men acquired for it new benefactions and placed its affairs on a sound footing.[3] Fisher saw the reward of his labours. Before he died Cheke and others had made the college famous as a home of Classical learning.[4]

The statutes which Fisher gave to the college in 1516 were identical with those already given to Christ's College. Nor did he hesitate in two revisions of this code to borrow freely, whether from his friend, Foxe, or his enemy, Wolsey.[5] In the college library is a copy of the Statutes of Corpus Christi College, Oxford, Foxe's 'beehive', underlined and

[1] *Early Statutes of St John's College*, ed. Mayor, J. E. B., 1530, cap. LIV.
[2] Fuller, T., *History of the University of Cambridge*, p. 227.
[3] Scott, Sir R. F. *op. cit.* III, pp. 362 ff.
[4] Ascham, R., *Scholemaster*, ed. Mayor, J. E. B., pp. 62, 158–62.
[5] The three codes are printed in *Early Statutes of St John's College*, ed. Mayor, J. E. B.

corrected, apparently in Fisher's hand. This was used in 1524 and the statutes of Cardinal College in 1530. Fisher's legislation is not markedly original. He incorporated those innovations in studies made elsewhere of whose importance he had become convinced. The provision in favour of the northern counties of England, which we have noted in the Statutes of Christ's, reappears in those of St John's. Hebrew and Greek were to be studied by those Fellows and scholars whom the Master and seniors thought suitable, and a lectureship in each of these languages was established in the college. One quarter of the Fellows were to undertake the duty of preaching to the people in English. These were the objects he had at heart—for the rest, the statutes in their lavish detail give a living picture of college life in the early sixteenth century.

For ten successive years Fisher had been elected Chancellor. In 1514, the University, with his approval, turned to Wolsey.[1] Wolsey spurned their obsequious approach, and the University, turning again to Fisher, chose him

[1] Hymers, J., *op. cit.* Appendix No. 8, p. 215 (Letter to Croke).

for life. It thus fell to him to hold office through years critical both for learning and religion.

The overthrow of scholasticism in the University was made by Henry VIII as a part of his dealings with the Church, but before that happened Fisher had opened the door to the New Learning. By his friendship with Erasmus, by his sympathy with the new Biblical criticism, by encouraging the study of Greek and by giving the classical renaissance 'a permanent home' in new colleges, he led Cambridge cautiously and peacefully towards the great change in academic studies.

Humanism for long aroused little interest in England. When Erasmus made his first visit in 1499, London, and not Oxford or Cambridge, was the chief centre where the New Learning was cultivated.[1] When he came a second time, in 1505, Cambridge, probably at Fisher's suggestion, offered him a doctor's degree.[2] Fisher had come to feel that Erasmus was 'necessary to our University',[3] and in

---

[1] Allen, P. S., *Age of Erasmus*, p. 128.
[2] Grace Book Γ, p. 46.
[3] *Erasmi Epist.* I, 485.

1511, drew him here to become Lady Margaret's Reader in Divinity. For a brief period Queens' College sheltered in its seclusion the most famous scholar of the Renaissance. Erasmus aimed to inspire in the rising generation a taste for better studies, to turn them from 'the dark riddles of Duns' to Greek, where they would find the 'well-springs of wisdom', 'copious rivers flowing over sands of gold.'[1] In October 1511, he began his lectures on the elements of Greek grammar. But his pupils were few and poor, the climate, the townsmen, the college ale, all disagreeable to him, and the divines preferred sophistical cavils to the historical method. The plague came, the University dispersed, and in 1514 Erasmus, disappointed of his hopes, departed. But he carried away the impression that, under Fisher's influence, Cambridge was adapting itself to the spirit of the age and ready to welcome the New Learning. 'It is scarcely thirty years ago', he wrote in 1516, 'when all that was taught in the University was Alexander (a school Latin grammar) the Little Logicals and those old

[1] Sandys, Sir J. E., *History of Classical Scholarship*, II, p. 230.

exercises out of Aristotle and quaestiones taken from Duns Scotus.' Now your University can compete with the leading Universities of our time. Students turn to the Gospels and Epistles instead of spending their lives on frivolous subtleties.[1] Late in life he still recalled those three colleges where youth was exercised not in dialectical wrestling matches but in true learning and sober argument.[2]

Greek had now come to stay, and, in 1519, Richard Croke, a member of King's College, was appointed Greek Reader. He began his inaugural with a reference to the Chancellor: 'What then is the message of my Lord of Rochester? Why, he exhorts them to apply themselves with all diligence to the study of Greek literature.... The exhortation of one who has never urged them to aught but what was most profitable.'[3] Fisher, besides sending a message, was setting an example. He himself now aspired to a knowledge of Greek, to the embarrassment of his friends who excused themselves from the task of teaching him.[4] In

---

[1] *Erasmi Epist.* II, 328.
[2] Mullinger, J. B., *The University of Cambridge*, I, 507.
[3] *Ibid.* p. 530. [4] *Erasmi Epist.* II, Nos. 520, 540.

1518 he also began the study of Hebrew. What progress he made in these languages we do not know.

While Oxford was divided by bitter feuds between Trojans and Graecians, the new learning made rapid headway in Cambridge, and particularly was Fisher's work bearing fruit in the colleges he had inspired. Ascham bears eloquent witness to this in the *Schole-master* and in his letters. Writing about 1542, he says, 'For some five years Aristotle and Plato had been studied at St John's; Sophocles and Euripides were more familiar than Plautus had been twelve years before; Herodotus, Thucydides and Xenophon were more "con-ned and discussed" than Livy was then; Demosthenes was as well known as Cicero; Isocrates as Terence; "it is Cheke's labours and example that have lighted up and continue to sustain this learned ardour".'[1]

So the New Learning took root and flourished in Cambridge, with far-reaching results for education in England. England was relieved from her dependence on Italy, and the way was opened for young men from the

[1] Sandys, Sir J. E., *op. cit.* II, 232.

blind alleys of scholasticism to a more spacious world. Fisher had made possible this marvellous progress. He had hastened what he might have hindered. He had extolled and established the learning that he lacked himself.

Fisher had reserved for his own use the Master's chambers in St John's. Letters and papers preserved in the college archives show with what close interest he watched its affairs. The accounts of his own foundations he seems generally to have audited. On the account for the year 1530–31 is the note: 'Of this £29. 9. 4¼ my lord allowed but £28. 9. 10¼ and the rest was deducted for Sir White and Matthew White (the Bishop's two scholars) sizing and for hose and shoes that they had more than my lord would allow.'[1] His famous library he gave to the college and by a special deed borrowed it during his life time, and in a private chapel, begun in 1524, he prepared his tomb.[2]

Meanwhile changes in the organisation and system of instruction in the University were proceeding apace.[3] The offices of Registrary

[1] Scott, Sir R. F., *op. cit.* IV, 35.   [2] *Ibid.* pp. 22–27, 30.
[3] Grace Book Γ, pp. xxi–xxvi.

and Public Orator were established. The caput for the supervision of graces makes its appearance. University printers were appointed. More care was taken of the Library. New endowments came in; the finances were satisfactory. The degrees given averaged over ninety a year. Mathematics was gaining an important place in the University curriculum.[1] The professional salaried lecturers were growing in number.[2] The printed book had come into the hands of students. In 1540 a scholar of St John's was executed for the murder of a townsman, the inventory of his effects shows that he had seven printed books—none, incidentally, was a Greek text.[3] The printed book transformed the duties of the lecturer. Instead of dictating a text he had now to expound it.[4]

What part the Chancellor took in these developments we do not know. But he was frequently called upon to assist in the perennial strife with the town which flared up again in the last decade of his life.[5] In 1534 both

[1] Grace Book B, p. xviii.   [2] *Ibid.* Part II, p. xix.
[3] Cooper, C. H., *op. cit.* I, 399.
[4] See *Report of the University Commission*, 1852, p. 46.
[5] Grace Book Γ, p. 287.

Universities renounced the right, so freely used against the Mayor, of excommunication in temporal causes.

While learning progressed as the Chancellor desired, the problems of religion in the University gave cause for increasing anxiety. To the end Fisher was outspoken in his condemnation of evils in the Church. What had bishops to do with princes' Courts, he asked, in the presence of Wolsey, in 1518.[1] Four years before the sack of Rome in 1527 he predicted divine judgment on the Pope and his Court if they did not reform themselves.[2] And in his treatise on Prayer he finds almost nothing left in the Church but open iniquity and pretended piety.[3] But he had no sympathy with the German Reformation. Neither he, nor More, would spare the heretic.[4] In the House of Lords he was vehement against laws that touched the privileges of the Church. But while her Chancellor in sermon and book was denouncing the Lutheran heresies, Cam-

---

[1] Mullinger, J. B., *op. cit.* I, 544.
[2] Bridgett, T. E., *op. cit.* p. 122; *Opera*, col. 653.
[3] Bridgett, T. E., *op. cit.* p. 435; *Opera*, col. 1715.
[4] *English Works of Sir Thomas More*, ed. Campbell, W. E., II, 319.

bridge was becoming a centre of discussion of the new doctrines. A famous inn was known as 'Germany'. Fellows of St John's, of King's and of Queens' Colleges stole in by night at the back door of the White Horse 'to discourse for edification in Christian knowledge'. Even the President of Queens' was to be found amongst them.[1] As the years passed it is clear that Fisher was feeling the Chancellorship a heavy burden and the spread of Lutheran opinions in the University grievously troubled him.[2] Did Cambridge want a Lutheran Chancellor, he asked in irony?

His great controversial writings belong to these years. Of all the books written against Luther at the beginning of the Reformation his were accounted the most important.[3] They circulated widely on the continent and the Pope pointed to them later as a ground for the Cardinalate.[4] But Fisher had not the light pen of Erasmus. These works remain as a monument of his vast learning, yet few perhaps

[1] Searle, W. G., *op. cit.* p. 172.
[2] Hymers, J., *op. cit.* pp. 215–16 (Letter to Croke).
[3] Acton, Lord, *Historical Essays*, p. 18.
[4] *Letters and Papers*, 1535, No. 777.

since the great religious struggle have turned their pages for pleasure or instruction.

It is otherwise with his English writings. He stands to the front in a generation that shaped our speech and gave us its thoughts in English prose. Each page calls up some scene of common life and reminds us that the writer is no Italianate ecclesiastic but English of the English. And he has at command an impressive rhetoric and craftsmanship with words.

In 1527 Fisher was at the height of his fame, esteemed not only the holiest bishop in the realm but England's foremost scholar. The King shared the general admiration. He believed that Fisher had not his equal in learning in Europe, and Reginald Pole, fresh from his Italian studies, was straitly questioned on the point. With some dexterous qualification, that conscientious scholar confirmed the King's opinion.[1] It was about this time that Holbein drew the honest, worn, ascetic face, which best reveals to us the man that Fisher was. In 1529 the University decreed for Fisher as a founder of colleges a perpetual dirge, an honour which,

[1] Strype, *Ecclesiastical Memorials*, III, Appendix, p. 246.

with due reference to the Lady Margaret, he welcomed, he said, with both hands.[1] But his reputation stood him now in ill stead. Those fateful stirrings of the royal conscience had begun, which shook and changed the polity of England. Soon all the foremost figures of the land were ranged on one or other side— chiefly on one—of the great controversy. Fisher's opinion would count in the King's great matter.

The question of the divorce was first broached to Fisher in general terms, and he appears to have made answer, as Lord Acton says, 'without suspecting that he was taking the first step on a road ending at the scaffold.'[2] Caution came when he saw the difficulties. But his side was chosen. Appointed one of the Queen's counsel, he became the champion, too eager for his own safety, of her cause. He has been called the rock of the English opposition to the divorce.[3] The metaphor is well chosen. The old man hardened like flint

---

[1] For the correspondence see Hymers, J., *op. cit.* Appendices Nos. 8–10, pp. 210–23.

[2] Acton, Lord, *op. cit.* p. 18.

[3] Pollard, A. F., *Wolsey*, p. 284.

against the royal wish. To oppose Henry in the prime of his great powers on the dearest object of his desire was a risk indeed terrible. The anger of the king is death, said Archbishop Warham.[1] But Fisher felt himself called to play the part of the Baptist.[2]

From the proceedings in the University about the divorce Fisher appears to have held aloof. But to no matter did he give so much study. The question on its merits, he admitted, might be difficult, but there was no question. The solution of doubts belonged to the Pope and the Pope had decided.[3] Always an indomitable fighter, Fisher pursued the hopeless contest. That he wrote books against the King and sent them abroad to be printed, that he advised the intervention of the Emperor, there seems no doubt.[4] Of these activities the Government knew only in part.

Events took their course, and in April 1533 Fisher was arrested to be kept out of the way while Cranmer pronounced the divorce and

---

[1] *Letters and Papers*, 1531–2, p. 137.
[2] *Ibid.* 1529–30, No. 5732.
[3] *Ibid.* 1526–8, IV, Pt. II, No. 3148.
[4] *Ibid.* 1533, pp. 407, 486, 511; Van Ortroy, p. 259.

the coronation of Anne was celebrated. A year later he refused the Oath of Succession and was sent to the Tower. In November 1534 refusal to acknowledge the King's headship of the Church was made treason by Act of Parliament. Large issues came here upon the horizon. The relations of Church and State, the grounds of political obedience, the functions and status of monarchy. Was obedience the foundation of all religious and social order? Was the power of Kings divine? So Gardiner, 'the ablest English jurist of his day', believed. But Fisher could not find, like Gardiner,[1] in an Act of Parliament the discharge of his conscience. 'Not that I condemn any other men's conscience,' he wrote to Cromwell, the new Secretary of State, 'their conscience may save them, and mine must save me.'[2]

Fisher lay in the Tower and Cromwell had noted in his 'remembrances'—'when Master Fisher shall go to execution'.[3] But his strength was failing and the course of nature might defeat the ends of the Government, for he had

[1] Muller, J. A., *Letters of Stephen Gardiner*, p. xxvii.
[2] *Letters and Papers*, 1534, No. 136; Lewis, *op. cit.* II, 402.
[3] *Letters and Papers*, 1535, No. 892.

not brought himself under the new Statute. On May 20, 1535, he was made a Cardinal. The Pope, misinformed about the state of things in England, believed that this promotion would protect him.[1] But it was the tall oaks that the King felled, and when the Chancellor Bishop became a Cardinal, his greatness challenged his fate. Trapped at last into denying the royal supremacy,[2] he brought himself under the new Treasons Act, of which he had no knowledge, and the penalty was death.

Through these trying years the University and the college stood by Fisher. St John's owed everything to him and owned it in his hour of peril.[3] The University had prudently reinsured its interests in high places. In 1533, an annual stipend was voted to Cromwell, 'our particular patron',[4] who was also elected High Steward. When the end had come they hastened to make their peace with the Government. To save themselves from harm, they

[1] *Vie du bienheureux martyr Jean Fisher*, ed. Van Ortroy, S.J., pp. 310–11.

[2] Hitchcock, E. V. and Chambers, R. W., *op. cit.* pp. 363–68.

[3] Lewis, J. *op. cit.* II, 356 (Letter from the College).

[4] Grace Book Γ, p. 286.

chose Cromwell to succeed Fisher as Chancellor and quietly accepted the Injunctions of 1535, which mark the downfall of scholasticism.

In St John's Cromwell commanded his arms to be defaced, and while the carpenters took down the fishes' heads in the Chapel,[1] the masons stopped their work on his tomb. Centuries later, when Mr Essex was casing the south side of the first court, his workmen came on an old tomb of clunch in a disused chapel, its parts elegantly shaped, but never connected together. It was Fisher's unfinished tomb, though not then recognised. Exposed to the weather, it perished within a year.[2] Nicholas Metcalfe, isolated and unhappy, was commanded by Cromwell to resign.[3] The library never came to the college. Cromwell dispersed it. 'They trussed up', says Fisher's biographer, 'XXXII great pipes, besides a number that were stolen away.'[4] Years later Ascham was still deploring the loss of 'this great treasure'.[5] From a new edition of the college statutes Fisher's name was dropped.

[1] Scott, Sir R. F., *op. cit.* IV, 281.
[2] *Ibid.* pp. 31–2.   [3] *Ibid.* III, p. 332.
[4] *Vie du bienheureux martyr Jean Fisher*, ed. Van Ortroy, S.J., p. 316.   [5] *Ibid.* pp. 124–5, 315.

Four centuries have now passed since More and Fisher died, and it is not likely that we shall know much more of them than we know now. Few figures in our national life have emerged as scatheless from the criticism of time. Oxford nurtured the one, and Cambridge the other: for some years Cambridge had them both—the one as High Steward, the other as Chancellor. They had carried forward the Renaissance in England, and England's Renaissance king struck them down. Fisher is endeared to every son of Cambridge by his services to collegiate life. In learning he mediated between the old and the new. On the stem of the medieval University he grafted the colleges of the Renaissance. The University has had no more faithful servant. Unsparing of effort, and ever loyal to its interests, he exalted the place of Cambridge in the national life. To the problems of Church and State he brought an unyielding integrity of mind and a character steeled in the austerities of the Middle Ages. For him the times were out of joint, but he surrendered neither faith nor courage. English liberty was not bound up with the preservation of papal power, yet if none had challenged Henry, how many would have resisted Charles? It is a key to his place in our history that in learning he promoted the work of Erasmus and in politics he shared the fate of More. His greater contemporary has left us his judgment: 'I reckon in this realm no one man in wisdom, learning and long approved virtue together, mete to be matched and compared with him.'[1] To the conduct and pattern of his life the Church which he defended and adorns has paid its highest tribute, and we, not less mindful of his virtue and service, in this Hall which knew his presence, remember to-day, with gratitude and humility, one who has placed us for ever in his debt.

[1] *Works of Sir Thomas More* (1557), p. 1437.